CORN-HUSK CRAFTS

LITTLE CRAFT BOOK SERIES

By **MARGERY FACKLAM**
& **PATRICIA PHIBBS**

 STERLING PUBLISHING CO., INC.   NEW YORK

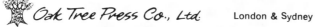 *Oak Tree Press Co., Ltd.*   London & Sydney

SAUNDERS OF TORONTO, Ltd., Don Mills, Canada

Little Craft Book Series

We wish to extend our appreciation and indebtedness to the many people who have helped with the material in this book:

To Clifford Schweikhard, J. Carl Burke, and Howard Facklam for their photographs; to Edith Cammack for her colorful dolls and many suggestions; and to Dr. Virginia Cummings, Director of the Buffalo Museum of Science, who let us loose in the corn fields.

MARGERY FACKLAM and PATRICIA PHIBBS

Contents

Before You Begin

Once a gift from the Indians, corn today is America's largest money crop. Almost every part of the corn stalk is used in making hundreds of products as diverse as baby powder and dynamite. Only the husk is left over. It was not a leftover to the Indians who used husks to weave sleeping mats, thatch roofs, insulate houses, weave moccasins, and make masks, baskets, and dolls. No wonder the ancient ancestors of the Indians from Peru to Canada used corn as a symbol of worship: corn supplied them with food, clothing, medicine, decoration, and household utensils.

Today, in some parts of the United States, there are people who use husks for mattress fillers, twist husks into cordage, and make chair bottoms, hats, and baskets of husks.

Now, when many of us are seeking a return to a waste-not, want-not philosophy, interest has been renewed in corn husks as a craft medium. What satisfaction you will get making something useful from a leftover!

The projects in this book are not complicated, and many of them can be made easily by children. While you may not be able to compete with an Appalachian craftsman, you will be able to make some decorative and useful items by the time you have learned what is contained in these pages.

Corn husks are tough. You can braid, wrap, twist, weave, fringe, curl, knot, or tie them. You can sew, cut, glue, paint, dye, or bleach them. You can use husks in almost as many ways as paper, and some ways in which paper cannot be used.

BUT, don't use corn husks as decorations around candles or as lamp shades. If you put corn-husk ornaments on your Christmas tree, keep them away from lights that might get hot. Husks burn easily and quickly.

Husks can be shaped into any form when wet, and they will retain that form when dry. They can be re-wet and you can start over.

But best of all, husks are free.

Materials for Corn-Husk Crafts

Scissors . . . old ones because they'll get wet.

String . . . kite string is good or dental floss or raffia (palm-leaf) strips. You can tie the doll with narrow strips of the husk itself, but it is difficult because the pieces are usually short. If you tie the doll with string, you can cover the string with corn husk or raffia.

Water in a bowl.

Corn husks.

These are the basic supplies, but for some other projects you may need glue, glycerin, fabric dye, and florist's wire and tape.

Illus. 1. The materials you need to work with husks are easy to find: a bowl of water, some string, and scissors. The glycerin, glue, and dye are inexpensive and easy to get.

The Corn Plant

The husk is the foliage of the corn or maize plant (*Zea mays*) that wraps the ear tightly in a protective coat. The fibres run lengthwise, parallel to the center vein, unlike the more brittle and less pliable leaf. Don't use the corn leaf for craft projects—it will split.

While you collect and save corn husks, keep some of the corn silk, too. You can use it for hair on dolls, and when you get tired of making dolls, you can steep 1 teaspoonful of finely cut silk in hot water, then strain and enjoy a cup of healthful tea. The Indians used to dry the silk and put it in broth to season and thicken it.

Where to Get Husks

There are two kinds of corn, sweet corn and field corn. You can use either one.

The sweet corn has whiter, finer inner husks which are better to use for dolls, wreaths, flowers, or detail work. The obvious way to get sweet-corn husks is to save those left over from your dinner. If you shop at one of those groceries where the produce man trims everything, ask for the husks which he will only throw away. Ask your friends to save husks for you, too, if they're not putting them on their compost heaps.

If you are near a farm where field corn (which is used for cattle feed and industrial processing) is available, you can collect that. The field-corn husks are larger and tougher, but they are durable for braided mats or baskets. Field-corn husks, while not quite as white as sweet-corn husks, can be bleached to whiten and soften them, however.

If you cut corn in the field, you will need a large plastic bag or basket for collecting and a sturdy knife to use on the ears that don't break off easily. If you are picking field corn, with the farmer's permission of course, husk it there and leave the cobs for his animals. That's what he grew it for.

In the late autumn when corn is dry and no longer edible, and before the farmers have cut it for their corn cribs, is the best time for collecting. You can use the husks immediately because they are dry and not green.

How to Dry Green Husks

If you have green husks they will have to be dried before you use them. Spread them on newspapers if you have room, or put them in a mesh laundry bag to hang where the air can circulate through them. If you don't have a mesh bag, make one from an old curtain or use an empty onion bag. Unless you live in the rain forests, the husks should be dry in a few days. As they dry, they will shrivel and curl. Don't worry. You have to work with them wet, and, when you wet them, the husks will return to their original shape and size.

If you have been working with the wet husks and decide to put them away for a while, repeat the drying process. If you store husks in a closed container while they still hold any moisture, they are sure to mildew.

How to Bleach Husks

Some of the corn you collect in the field will be spotted from fungus and rust, but you can bleach

these husks and at the same time make them softer. If you have only field-corn husks, try bleaching them to use in place of sweet-corn husks.

Here's how: put a quarter of a cup of liquid laundry bleach in a large mixing bowl full of water. Add the husks, making sure you cover them with the water. Half an hour is usually enough, but check frequently to see if the spots are disappearing. The less time in the bleach the better—rinse them in clear water before proceeding.

An Indian Doll

As many recipes exist for making corn-husk dolls as for apple pie. No two Indian families made them exactly alike, and you will probably find ways of making your doll unique after you learn the basic steps.

Soak a bunch of about a dozen husks in a bowl of water for a few minutes. The entire process will be worked with wet husks. Choose six large husks and lay them on top of each other with the wide edge at the top as in Illus. 4.

About an inch from the top, gather the husks and tie them tightly (Illus. 5). Cut off the top of the husks, and round it into a head as in Illus. 6.

Holding the head in your hand, peel one end of each husk down over the other, like a banana, pulling firmly and smoothly (Illus. 7). Don't be afraid to pull—the husks are tough. If the head turns out to be smaller than you intended, roll up

Illus. 2. This Seneca Indian doll with bead necklace and yarn hair was made from directions like those given here for a primitive Indian doll.

7

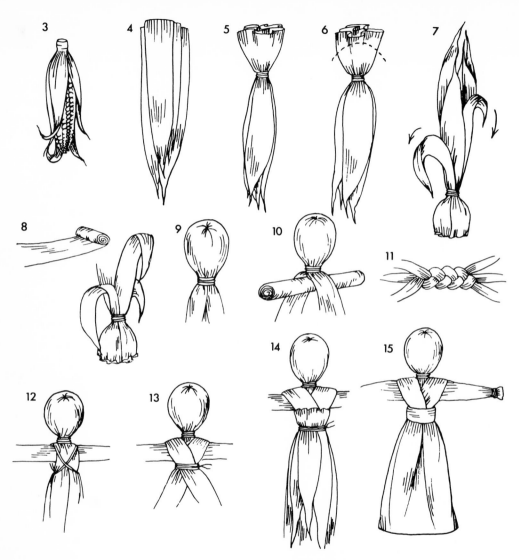

Illus. 3-15. Steps in making a doll.

another piece of husk and push it inside the folded-down husks to add to the size (Illus. 8). Tie the husks to make a neck like that shown in Illus. 9.

Make the arms now from two husks rolled together one on top of the other into a long piece and inserted between the ends of the head husks as in Illus. 10.

Separate the ends of the husks that extend below the head and pull them firmly apart. Place the arm roll tightly against the tied neck.

Some people like braided arms (Illus. 11) instead of rolled ones. They are also easy to make. Just tie three husks at the top and braid them, tying off the ends. Insert the braid just like the rolled arms.

Tie the arms in place with a criss-cross over the chest and back as in Illus. 12. Don't tie the ends of

the arms yet, even though they are obviously too long. Wait until the doll is otherwise finished so you can trim the arms in proportion to the doll's height. Now take two more husks and fold each one into a strip about an inch wide. These will be the shoulders. Place one over each shoulder position and cross them over the chest and back, as in Illus. 13. Tie these pieces tightly around the waist.

The Skirt

One kind of skirt is made of long, wide husks laid on well above the waistline, as in Illus. 14, tied tightly and trimmed so that the excess will not show above the waistband. For this, fold another husk into a band about 1 inch wide and tie it over the skirt top, as in Illus. 15. Cut off the skirt at a length proportionate to the doll's size. Then bend the arms down and cut them off at a point about one third of the way down the skirt.

(If you decide to turn this doll into a male, just separate the skirt, wind the husks around the legs, and bend the ends of the legs up for feet.)

If you let the doll dry now, the skirt will flare out and the arms will stick out like a scarecrow. Bend the arms any way you like, perhaps folded as though holding something, and tie them loosely until they dry. Put a loose string around the skirt to hold it in place until it dries. Once dry, the doll will retain its shape.

Illus. 16. To make a full, gathered skirt for your doll, put the husks on around the waist with the broad end over the head. When all the husks have been gathered around the waist and tied snugly, pull the husks down to make the skirt.

9

For a fuller, gathered skirt, put the husks in place as shown in Illus. 16. With the wide part of the husk on top, the pointed end will extend about 2 inches below the waistline. Gather six or seven husks around the waist and tie them firmly. Then pull down the husks into a skirt. Tie it in place and let it dry.

The Indians of the great Iroquois nation of the Northwest never put faces on their dolls in the old days, although some do now for the tourist trade. They tell Indian children the legend of the faceless doll. It seems that the first corn-husk doll was made as a companion for children, but she was so beautiful that she spent all her days looking at herself in a clear pool in the forest. The Creator did not want children to learn to be so vain, and he took away the doll's face forever.

A Character Doll

With a few variations in method you can make a corn-husk doll that is not as stiff-looking as the primitive Indian doll, one that actually conveys a feeling of motion and grace.

Begin by making the head as for the Indian doll with six husks laid on top of each other. Put two of the whitest husks you have in the middle of the stack, because these will become the face. Gather and tie the husks an inch from the top. Trim the ends into a rounded shape for the head. Pull the husks, banana-like, and tie the neck.

Pull two husks up over the head to be used for the bodice later. Pull one husk to each side for the arms. And leave two husks straight down for the legs or skirt (Illus. 17).

To make the hand, take a narrow husk and roll it between your thumbs and forefingers so it will twist. When you fold this twisted piece in half it will twist further and make a loop to be used for the hand. Lay the hand in the arm husk which you have trimmed as in Illus. 19.

Fold the shortened arm husk around the hand

Illus. 18. For this modern corn-husk doll, the hair was made from un-ravelled twine.

and wrap it tightly with a narrow strip of husk from wrist to shoulder (Illus. 20). Tie it at the shoulder. Make the other arm and the legs exactly the same way.

Puffed Sleeve

To make the puffed sleeve you see on many of the Czechoslovakian corn-husk dolls, look at Illus. 21 as you put a husk, broad end toward the body, under the wrapped arm. Gather the husk around the arm and tie it between the elbow and wrist. Pull the pointed end of the sleeve husk up toward the shoulder, puffing and rounding it into shape. Tie it near the shoulder. Do NOT trim it. It should look like Illus. 22, when finished.

Next, fold a piece of husk into a small package, enough to fill out the chest of the doll. Lay it under the doll's neck and wrap the ends of the

sleeves you did not trim over and around the chest filling. Still holding this in place, bring down the two husks that have been pulled up over the head to cover the chest and back. Tie these securely at the waist.

Finishing

Put on the doll's skirt as you did the Indian doll's. When you trim the skirt be careful not to cut off the legs. You can pin the skirt to look as though the wind blew it.

If your doll will spend the rest of its time sitting on a log, or kneeling to pick a flower, or flying on your Christmas tree as an angel, or ice skating, now is the time to decide. While the doll is wet you can turn its head, bend its arms, legs, waist, or knees.

Take a piece of wood or whatever will be the doll's base and place the doll on it. Looping string around the figure, tie the head, arms, and legs into place, pinning where necessary. In a day or two when the doll is dry, remove the string and pins. If you don't like the way it dried, dip the doll in water and begin again.

The Little Extras

The variations you can make on a basic doll are what make this hobby fun. For an angel, cut

Illus. 20. Wrap a narrow piece of husk around the arm to hold the hand in place.

Illus. 21. To make a puffed sleeve, place a husk in this position and tie it at the center of the arm. Then fold it toward the body, rounding and shaping it.

Illus. 22. The puffed sleeve should look like this when finished.

wings from graceful-looking corn husks and add a bit of tinsel for a halo. If you want a more frilly angel, shred the skirt. While the skirt is wet, take a needle and pierce the husk, pulling the needle quickly downward with the grain of the husk. Do this all around the skirt until it is finely shredded. When it dries, the skirt will be very curly and fluffy-looking.

Glue on corn silk or unravelled twine or yarn for hair. Or make tiny braids of corn husks to use for pigtails or a matronly bun. Add an apron, a bonnet, a scarf or a hat. Put a bunch of miniature

dried flowers or a tiny corn husk baby in the doll's arms.

For one of the most unusual gifts you can make, try corn-husk figures to illustrate your friends' hobbies or professions. Put a corn-husk teacher behind a small dollhouse-size desk with a pointer in one hand, a book in the other. Make a corn-husk grandmother who will sit in a small rocker as she knits.

Time is well invested when you make corn-husk dolls because they will last longer than your lifetime.

13

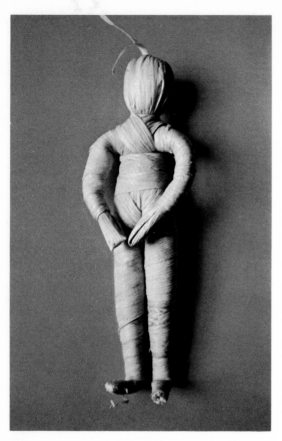

Illus. A. To make a male doll, wrap the legs like those of this Seneca Indian doll. (Instructions on page 7.)

Illus. B. These skaters show the extent of motion you can convey with corn-husk dolls and a way to illustrate a hobby.

Illus. C. "Boys on a Raft" will give you an idea of the variety and detail you can create with husks.

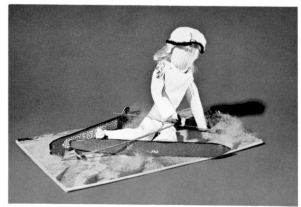

Illus. D. What better get-well gift for an injured skiing friend than this corn-husk creation?

Illus. 23. This Seneca Indian warrior was made of husks.

Illus. 24. This tiny Mexican doll on a corn-cob base has a nose made from a knotted piece of husk. Directions for making the nose are the same as those for making a bird's beak (page 40).

How to Dye Husks

Most corn-husk projects look best in natural color, but there are times you may want other tones. For bright and vibrant shades use commercial fabric dye. Put two teaspoons of dye into a large mixing bowl and add very hot water. Add one or two drops of liquid dish detergent, which seems to soften the husks so that they take the dye more evenly. Or you can add a small lump of alum instead of the detergent.

Put the husks in the dye bath, making sure they are all covered. Stir them once in a while as you check for the shade you want. For a light tint, it is often enough just to dip the husks in and out of the dye bath a few times. For deeper shades leave the husks in an hour or more. Rinse the husks thoroughly under cool running water before you use them. And wear plastic gloves unless you like green fingers.

For more subtle, earthy tones it's fun to try natural dyes. Probably you have a few valuable

Illus. F. An effective decorating accessory is a shadow box using one of your corn-husk dolls.

Illus. E. Corn-husk dolls can even have moveable joints as this gingham-dressed girl has.

Illus. H. A natural-color fringed tree. The husks will curl as they dry.

Illus. G. This Christmas tree was made with narrow strips of husks which had been dyed, put into groups of three, wired and attached to a Styrofoam base.

dyes in your kitchen now, without knowing it. Try onion skins to dye husks a deep rust color, or beet juice for a rich red. Grapes will give you a beautiful purple, and blueberries, of course, turn out blue. These give up their color almost immediately. Turmeric, a herb in the ginger family, can be used for a deep yellow dye.

The marigolds in your garden, or dahlias, or zinnias, when boiled in water, will yield shades from rust to lemon-yellow. Poplar leaves make a buttery yellow dye, and black walnut hulls can be cooked into a rich black dye. When using plants, whether it be its leaf, flower, root, or bark, fresh or dry, crush or break it and let it stand overnight in water. Then boil the plant parts until the color begins to emerge. Poplar leaves and walnut hulls have to be boiled for hours. Don't forget to add the alum or detergent.

Rinse dyed husks well before you use them.

Make a Green Tree

A small Christmas tree on a Styrofoam (stiff plastic foam) cone base is a quick and easy project to make with dyed husks. Dye a bowlful of husks with commercial green dye. Rinse them well.

Illus. 25 (left). How to loop a husk. Illus. 26 (right). After your groups of three husks are wired together, push them into the plastic foam tree base beginning at the bottom.

For the tree in color Illus. G (page 19), you will need florist's wire, the dyed husks, the Styrofoam cone, and a few small pine cones or red berries.

Tear the husks into 1-inch-wide strips. Fold a strip over into a loop (Illus. 25). Tie three of these loops together by winding a short piece of wire around the base of the loops. Leave one half inch of wire sticking out. Push the wire into the plastic

Illus. 27. How to fold the husks for the tailored tree.

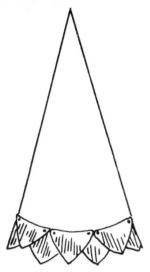

Illus. 28. Pin the folded husks on the cone beginning at the bottom and overlapping them as you work toward the top.

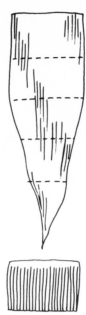

Illus. 29. Cut the husks into 2-inch cross-sections and fringe them with a needle while they are wet.

cone, starting at the bottom (Illus. 26) and filling the cone with green loops. Put them close together—the husks will dry and shrink. Push wire through the small pine cones and push them between the loops.

Another Kind of Tree

Using the same kind of Styrofoam cone as a base, you can make a trim, tailored kind of tree in natural husks, highlighted with a touch of antique gold spray.

Cut out a 2-inch square of husk. Fold it into one triangle and fold that triangle again (Illus. 27). While this folded husk is still wet, pin it to the

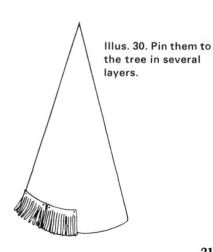

Illus. 30. Pin them to the tree in several layers.

21

Illus. J. This ceremonial mask of the Iroquois Indian nation was made of braided husks sewn together with fringe added.

Illus. K. A sturdy door mat can be made from braided sections sewn together.

Illus. L (below). This wreath, made of groups of three loops tied together and attached to a frame, is trimmed with pine cones, milkweed pods and a small make-believe bird.

Illus. M (above). Shredding the husks makes a different kind of wreath.

base of the cone. Keep adding new triangles, overlapping them to hide the pins (Illus. 28).

And Still Another Tree

You'll need another of those Styrofoam cones and more pins for this tree. This time cut out 2-inch squares of husks and fringe them with a needle. Pierce the husk and pull the needle down with the grain of the husk. This will shred the husks (Illus. 29), and they will curl as they dry. Beginning at the base, pin them to the cone as in Illus. 30. Work to the top of the cone, overlapping several layers for a curly-looking tree (Color Illus. H on page 19).

How to Soften and Preserve Husks

Florists, museum display experts, and those in the business of preserving plants know the value of glycerin as a plant preservative. If you have ever used rose water and glycerin on your hands you know of glycerin's softening quality. It works on corn husks, too.

For making dolls or wreaths that are only to look at, it doesn't matter if the husks dry and become brittle. But a corn-husk article that will get more use will last longer if it does not turn brittle. Also, husks soaked in a glycerin solution are easier to braid and fold.

Illus. 31. When you add a piece of husk in a braid, fold it around the strand you are adding it to.

24

You can buy glycerin in any pharmacy. It's not expensive. Add 2 or 3 teaspoons of glycerin to a large mixing bowl of water in which you are soaking husks. The glycerin will permeate the husk so that, as it dries, the husk retains some of the pliability it had while fresh.

Braided Wreaths

Use glycerin-soaked husks to braid this wreath. Take three large, white husks and tie or staple them together at the top of the husk. Hook the bunch of husks over a nail or have a patient friend

Illus. 32. Corn husks can be braided and sewn into a circle for coasters or table mats.

hold it as you braid. Use the whole husks for a thick braid or narrower strips for a skinny braid.

Because the husks are short, you often have to add pieces. Overlap the ends as you add new strips (Illus. 31) and alternate the additional strands so that you don't have all three pieces joined at about the same spot.

If you are making a small, flat wreath you can join the ends in a circle with a staple, or tie the ends together while the wreath is wet. When the wreath dries, glue or wire pine cones, teasel flowers, milkweed pods or ribbon over the joined place.

The wreath in color on the back cover is a small one used for a kitchen window decoration. To make a large braided wreath for an outside door use several thicknesses of husks. Tie the beginning and end of the braid with tough cord. Wire on pine cones and water-resistant ribbon. Rain or snow won't hurt your corn-husk wreath.

Illus. N. You can make a sturdy mat by starting with a length of rope and winding it around as you go. You coil the covered rope and bind the coil with corn husk strips, until you have a circular mat.

Illus. O. This mat has been made by wrapping and coiling husks along with some long grass and sewing them together.

Illus. P. If you build the coils up on a base and on each other, you can make a basket. The sides of this one are sewn together.

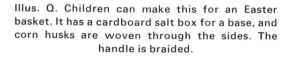

Illus. Q. Children can make this for an Easter basket. It has a cardboard salt box for a base, and corn husks are woven through the sides. The handle is braided.

Other Braided Projects

Braided husks can be turned into a variety of useful things. Narrow braids are easily sewn together in a circle as in Illus. 32 to make coasters or table mats.

Small baskets, like the miniature one in Illus. 33 are simple to put together. Braid narrow pieces and, instead of sewing them flat, build the sides up into the shape you have in mind. Sew a braided handle in place.

You can braid pieces to sew into a sandal, too, but they are bumpy for bare feet. The Indians made moccasins of corn husks (pictured in color on the front cover) which were worn inside a deerskin boot the way hunters today use an insulated sock inside a boot. Inside the corn-husk moccasin they put a soft mullen leaf or other soft fibre for comfort. But if you want to make a sandal, just sew strips of braid into a shoe-sole shape. Add a wide band of braided husks for a strap over the arch, or sew on leather thongs which will be tied around the ankle.

If you sew narrow corn-husk braids together in parallel strips you can make a place mat. Or fold it into a pouch purse which you can attach to a wooden handle. You would have to line it with bright calico or mattress ticking.

Illus. 33. The basket held in the doll's braided arms is made of narrow strips of husks braided and sewn together.

Corn Underfoot

If you feel all thumbs making small articles, try making a door mat. It's sturdy, useful, and goes together quickly. You don't have to fuss with hiding loose ends—in fact, the whole idea is to have lots of loose ends.

Use large field-corn husks. Tie three damp husks together at the top. Begin a braid, but each time you fold a strand over, add a new husk, letting 2 inches of the new piece extend out of the braid (Illus. 34). Add a new husk with each fold so that the new husks will stick out on alternating sides, making tufts (Illus. 35). Use the newly attached husk in the braid by doubling it with one of the original husks. This way only the ends of the new husk should protrude.

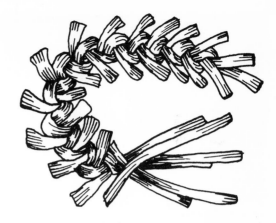

Illus. 35. Making a door mat.

When the braid measures 18 inches, tie it off and begin a new one. You will need 10 or 12 braids. Lay them together with the tufts of the first strip laying in one direction and the next strip in the opposite direction, alternating each braid.

While the thick braids are still wet, sew them together on the smoothly braided side with heavy cord and a large darning needle. Pull the braids tightly because they loosen as they dry. Turn the mat tuft-side up and trim the tufts evenly. (See Color Illus. K, page 22.)

Put the mat in place at the front door. When it wears out, throw it away. For a few hours work and the cost of thread, you can have a fresh new mat each autumn.

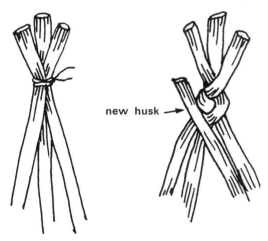

new husk →

Illus. 34. How to add pieces into a braid for tufted effect.

Illus. R. Birds, made like the first few steps of the doll, can be converted into mobiles or displayed as decorations.

Illus. S. The face of the lamb is built like that of the bird, but the snout is tied to indent it as it dries. Twigs were used for legs and curls of husks were glued on.

Illus. T. This hound dog was made from a wire base wrapped in corn husks by Appalachian craftsmen.

Looped Wreath

Set against wood panelling or in an informal room, a corn-husk wreath is a Christmas decoration you are not likely to see in every house in town.

The same method of looping husks that you used to make the small Christmas tree is the way to make the wreath.

Wet the husks. Use strips about 2 inches wide. Fold a strip into a loop and put three or four loops in one group. You can wire the husks together and push the wire into a Styrofoam wreath base. Or you can tie the loops together and secure them to a wire or rattan frame. The wreath in Color Illus. L (page 23) was tied to a rattan frame.

Really pack the loops in because as they dry they shrink. Remember? And you don't want a scraggly wreath.

Corn husks alone can be drab, so add pine cones or dried milkweed pods or teasel flowers. Highlight the color with a little antique gold spray or clear lacquer. A red calico ribbon or clusters of dried rose hips or red berries is a nice touch.

Fringed Wreath

For a wreath like the one in Color Illus. M (page 23), you need a coat hanger or other wire of similar size which can be curved into a circle, along with masking tape and many husks. After you have made a circle of wire, tape it together.

Look at Illus. 36 to see how to loop the husks onto the wire frame. You make a loop and lay it under the frame with the loop on the outside of the wreath. Take the tail of the loop and bring it over the wire and through the loop so that it knots. Pack these husks in as tightly as you can.

When the frame is completely covered, use a needle to shred the husks (as before) beginning next to the frame and pulling the needle out to the edge with the grain of the husk. When the husks are all fringed, cut them evenly and spread them out with your hand. Hang the wreath up to dry.

Wire on some pine cones or an acorn-husk bird (see page 42) or berries or a ribbon to decorate your wreath.

Illus. 36. Fold a husk in half and loop it around a wire ring to make a fringed or shredded wreath.

Illus. V. These corn flowers and tiny dogwood blossoms have been made from colorfully dyed husks.

Illus. U. The carnation-like flower was made by shredding the husks while they were wet. The zinnia-type flower in front has a center made of a Styrofoam ball painted brown and slit to make places to glue in the petals. The flower in the rear is made from a teasel with corn-husk petals.

Illus. W. You can make large, dramatic sunflowers like this from husks dyed yellow.

Illus. 37. This owl should be an easy project for children, because it only requires cutting out pieces of husk and glueing them to a firm background material.

Corn-Husk Sculpture

Paper sculpture is a craft used by elementary school children, professional artists and every level of ability in between. Effective for posters and bulletin boards, it is also popular for framed pictures and greeting cards. You can produce more interesting sculptures if you use husks instead of paper because of the husks' texture and color variations. The only thing you have to consider differently is the size of your work. Corn husks are small and your sculpture should be easily adaptable to small pieces. For this project you will need only glue and a background board, besides the husks.

Sketch your design and decide what technique you want to use to build your picture. Looped husks can represent the tails of birds, tree tops, flowers, or clouds. Shred the husks, twist them or fold them for variation. To curl husks, wrap a wet strip of husk around a pencil and hold it in place with a thumb tack while it dries. Pull it out into a curl that will last until it is re-wet.

The owl in Illus. 37 uses only cut-out scraps of husks. Some were allowed to dry and curl and others were dried under a weight so they would not curl. Children can make corn husk sculptures with great imagination.

A Coiled Mat

As you work on an apparently simple coiled mat, you will appreciate the dexterity and patience of the Indian women who made durable, attractive baskets and mats for their household utensils. Using either long grasses or rolled corn husks for the core of the work, they wrapped narrow strips of husks around that core, coiling and sewing it together as the work grew in size.

The easiest way for you to learn to make a coiled mat is to begin with rope as the center or core instead of grass or husks. Then you can learn to cope with the short ends that stick out and not have to worry about keeping the core round and firm at the same time. When you know how to make a rope-center coil, you can try making a mat with a corn-husk core wrapped in raffia. Raffia is a fibre made from a species of palm, used mainly for weaving, and can be purchased at a craft supply shop.

The raffia is the same color as husks, but it is in easier-to-work strands for wrapping and sewing. And finally, having learned to wrap and cope with a husk core too, you can make a mat completely of husks. But first, start with the rope as a core.

You'll need a length of clothesline or thicker

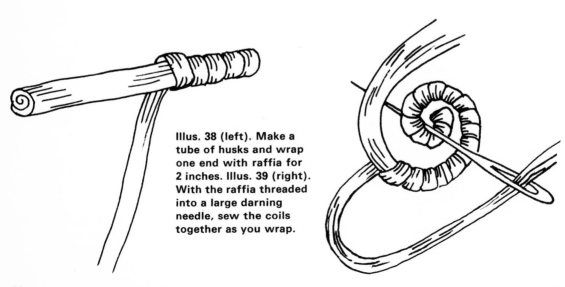

Illus. 38 (left). Make a tube of husks and wrap one end with raffia for 2 inches. Illus. 39 (right). With the raffia threaded into a large darning needle, sew the coils together as you wrap.

Illus. 40. When using raffia for wrapping the husks, be sure you make the coil tight.

rope if you want a thicker mat; corn husks dampened and torn in 2-inch strips; and a blunt stick such as an ice-cream stick or coffee stirrer which you will use for poking stray ends into the coil.

Wrap the end of the rope for 2 inches. Then press the wrapped end into the beginning of a coil. You have to hold the coil and wrapping husks firmly (see Color Illus. N, page 26). You will wish you had three hands on this project. Because the husks are short, you have to add a piece every few inches. After four or five times around the rope with the husk, take the husk around the previous coil, pushing it through with the stick and fastening the two circles together. Continue in this way until the mat reaches the size you want or you run out of

patience. The end of the coil must be tapered off and sewn on to make an even finish. Trim the rope into a tapered point before you wrap it at the end. If you stop work for a while and the mat dries, dip it in water before you start to work again.

More Coiled Mats

After the rope-filled mat, are you ready to try the husk-filled mat? You'll need husks, a darning needle, and raffia.

This time you roll two husks together into a tube, like a pencil (Illus. 38). Begin wrapping the end of the rolled husks as you did the rope, using wet raffia. Twist the wrapped husks into a tight coil and sew them together with the wrapping raffia as in Illus. 40.

When the core husks come to an end, add a new roll of husks by putting it well inside the roll in use. As you wrap them with the raffia, the new husks will stay in place. When your raffia thread gets short, pull it through the husk core and cut it off, leaving an inch or so sticking out.

Start a new piece of raffia by putting it through the center of the core (Illus. 39) and leaving an end of it extending an inch. Lay the ends of the old and the new piece of raffia along the husk core. They will be covered.

By using colored raffia you can create patterns as you wrap and sew coils together. This kind of mat is sturdy and, if it gets wet, it won't be damaged.

And Then the All-Husk Mat

When you think you have mastered the wrapping and coiling, you might like to try a mat made completely of husks. The only thing that makes such a mat more difficult than the others is the fact that the husks are short and you are constantly adding new ones.

You make a roll of the husks and wrap it with narrow strips of other damp husks, attaching the coils to each other as you did in the other mats. Keep the husks wet, pull the wrapping as tight as you can, and if you stop work before the mat is finished, pin the ends to a piece of cardboard so they will not unravel. Wet the whole mat to begin again.

Coiled Basket

To expand your coiled mat into a basket, just keep wrapping. But when you have coiled the size you want for the base of the basket, it is time to begin building the sides. All you do is move the layers of coils on top of each other. These coils can be sewn together with heavy thread or raffia, or bound together with the wrapping husks as you did in the mat.

A handle is simply another piece of rope wrapped in husks, and sewn in place. The handle

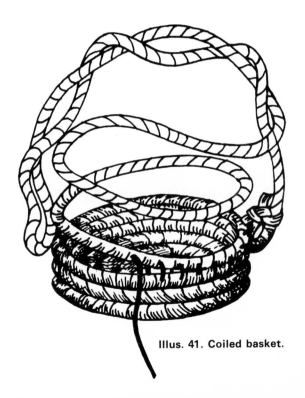

Illus. 41. Coiled basket.

in Color Illus. P, page 27, was a continuation of the top basket coil looped over, sewn in place, and then twisted around itself to be sewn again on the opposite side. You slant the sides of the basket in or out by the way in which you lay the coils on each other.

Salt-Box Woven Basket

Corn husks are not commonly used to weave baskets because the husks are short and longer grasses are more efficient to use. The basket in Color Illus. Q, page 27, was made by using an empty cylindrical cardboard salt box as the base for weaving.

Cut the salt box in half. Cut the sides into one-half inch strips from top to bottom, at right angles to the bottom, being careful to leave them attached firmly at the bottom. You can cover the box base with strips of corn husk glued on, or you can weave a tightly packed covering of husks which will cover the cardboard.

Twist a length of husk and begin to weave it in and out of the cardboard strips of the cut box. When you add a new husk, make sure it is tucked under the previous husk. Keep pushing the husks down together because they will loosen as they dry. (But you have heard that before.) Continue weaving until you cover all the cardboard strips.

Braid or twist a handle and sew it on. Cover the bottom of the basket, inside and out, with a large husk trimmed to fit. This makes a simple and serviceable Easter basket for children to make. Of course you can't get it wet because of the cardboard inside.

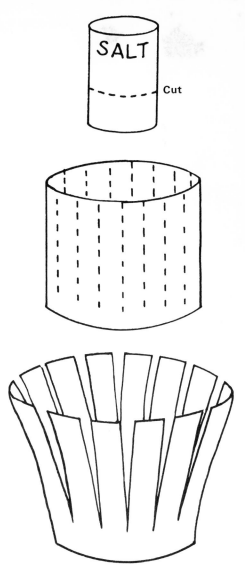

Illus. 42. Plan for salt-box woven basket.

Another Easy Basket

Using the method of folding squares of husks into triangles illustrated in the Christmas tree section (page 16), you can build another basket on a box base. A sturdy cardboard box or milk carton cut down, husks, and glue or a stapler are all you need. Staple or glue the triangles of husks in overlapping layers to the box. Around the top edge of the basket you will need to glue a braided or twisted strip of husks to finish it neatly.

Make a Bird

A corn-husk bird can fly on your Christmas tree, become part of a mobile or decorate a wreath. (See Color Illus. R, page 30.)

You begin as you did for the doll (page 6). Place five or six husks together and tie them about one inch from the top. Round off the top inch to shape the head and pull the husks, banana style, over the head. Some people like to use a small Styrofoam ball or a wooden bead as the core for a very round head.

Before you tie the neck you have to add the beak. A beak may look complicated, but it's as easy as tying a knot. Do just that (Illus. 43). Take a 1-inch-wide strip of husk and slowly tie a knot in it. Before tightening the knot, press it with your fingers to shape and flatten it into a more pointed shape. Then place this knotted beak on the front of the bird's head and tie it in with the neck.

All the ends of the husks from the head will form the body and tail. If it looks as though your bird is going to be scrawny, you may want to

stuff it. Again, you can use a Styrofoam ball for a round body, but it's just as easy to add some corn-husk padding and pull the ends of the husks down over that padding and tie them. Cut the tail straight across or into a V shape. Look at a bird picture book to see what kinds of tails birds have.

Cut out two wings from another husk and glue them on. With a needle, thread a string through the bird's back if you are going to use it for an ornament or a mobile.

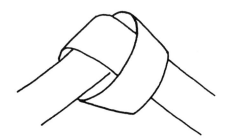

Illus. 43. Tie a knot this way in a narrow strip of husk to form the bird's beak.

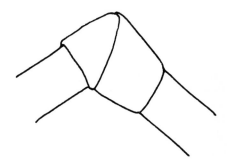

Illus. 44. Pipe-cleaner outline of a lamb.

Animals

If you make a framework or armature of pipe cleaners or wire, it is easy to build almost any animal. Twist two pipe cleaners together into a body and legs leaving an end for the tail and making a loop for the head. Using narrow, damp strips of husks begin to wrap the pipe cleaners tightly starting at the bottom of the feet and tail and up around the body. Use string to tie the husks in place so they won't unwind. Wrap husks around the chest, between the legs, building up the body and covering all the pipe cleaners.

The top layers of the husks should be tied only until they dry and then any loose ends can be glued down. Cut out husk ears or use scraps of felt for ears. Some people like to use a felt-tip ink marker to make the eyes, but you can make them by cutting a very thin slice of a narrow plastic tube. Glue it on the animal's face and put a dot of black paint in the center of the eye and a dab of pink on the nose.

To make the curly covering of a lamb (Color Illus. S on page 30) or a poodle or the tail of a pig, tear a very narrow strip of husk and wind it around a toothpick while it's wet. Put a pin or thumbtack in it until it dries. Then pull out the dry curl and wind it around the animal's body fastening it with glue. The hound dog (Color Illus. T on page 31) is a fine example of craftsmanship.

43

Do-It-Yourself Flowers

Real flowers are like real diamonds or fur. They have a quality which no man-made fibre can quite equal. Even artificial flowers made from natural materials have some of that unknown quality and texture that cold, lifeless plastic can imitate but not replace.

Corn-husk flowers are easy enough for children to make, but they offer enough variety for the most creative adult. Many patterns for paper flowers can be adapted to corn husks.

Zinnias

Begin with a simple zinnia-like flower made from all natural materials. You'll need a dried teasel (look at Illus. 45 if you don't know what a teasel is), a few husks, and white (Elmer's) glue.

Be careful of the prickly stem of the teasel. Either hold it with a paper towel as you work or take the blade of your scissors and gently scrape off the prickers before you start the flower.

Illus. 45. Cut off the dried teasel (center) to look like the one on the right. Then cut petals from husks and glue them into the teasel, so your flower will look like the one on the left.

44

Cut off the top of the teasel, leaving a $\frac{1}{2}$-inch to $\frac{3}{4}$-inch base. Cut the husks into petal shapes. A pattern is suggested in Illus. 46 but you can make the petals round or long and narrow, or any way you like them. Dip the end of each petal in glue and stick the petal between the layers of the teasel base.

Just the slightest bit of antique Flemish finish spray paint or antique gold on the petals will add a shine. If you want colored flowers, begin with dyed husks. The rust onion-skin dye and the poplar-leaf yellow (see page 16) are particularly nice for make-believe zinnias. (See Color Illus. U on page 34.)

Illus. 46. Pattern for a petal.

Carnations

For a carnation-like flower you will need four or five husks, some florist's wire for wrapping the flower, a stiffer wire for the stem (No. 18 gauge is good), green florist's tape, and string.

If you want a black center for your flower, dye a husk or color it with a felt-tip ink marker before you begin. In Illus. 47, you can see how to roll the black husk into a tube the size of a pencil, and roll a natural colored husk around the black one. About 1 inch from the end of the roll twist a piece of the fine wire tightly. Cut off the roll of husk about a half inch below the wire. Save the rest of the rolled husk for other flower centers. Bend the wire ends straight down from the center.

Now take a needle and pierce the husk and pull the needle quickly out to the edge through the grain of the husk. This will shred the flower center.

Cut other damp husks cross-wise in 2- or 3-inch lengths. Gather or pleat each of these pieces around the center of the flower, overlapping them as you add each one. When the flower is as thick as you want it, tie the base with string. Again use the needle to shred the petals as you did for the center. Let the flower stand upside down as it dries so the petals spread out. When it is dry, push a piece of heavier wire into the bottom of the flower center for a stem. Using the green florist's tape, wrap the base of the flower and the stem in a diagonal spiral.

Corn-husk carnations are attractive additions to your dried flower arrangements. (See Color Illus. U on page 34.)

Delphiniums

Dye the husks with commercial blue dye. Cut oval-shaped petals of husk about 2 inches long and 1 inch wide. Next fold a length of florist's wire in half. Take three petals at a time and gather them into the center of the wire loop. Twist the wire tightly around the petals to form the first blossom.

Continue gathering three petals together, alternating down the stem by using first the left, then the right end of the wire. Bunch the blossoms up closely to each other to make the flower nice

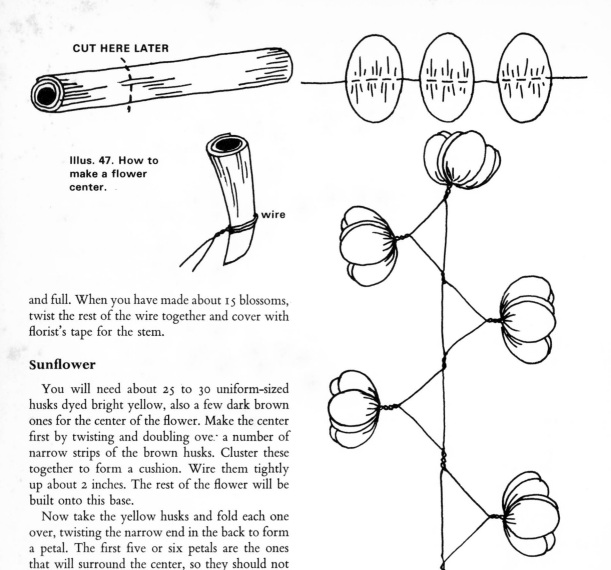

CUT HERE LATER

Illus. 47. How to make a flower center.

wire

and full. When you have made about 15 blossoms, twist the rest of the wire together and cover with florist's tape for the stem.

Sunflower

You will need about 25 to 30 uniform-sized husks dyed bright yellow, also a few dark brown ones for the center of the flower. Make the center first by twisting and doubling over a number of narrow strips of the brown husks. Cluster these together to form a cushion. Wire them tightly up about 2 inches. The rest of the flower will be built onto this base.

Now take the yellow husks and fold each one over, twisting the narrow end in the back to form a petal. The first five or six petals are the ones that will surround the center, so they should not be too long. Wire these to the top of the base. Continue to work several circles of petals,

Illus. 48. Gathering and clustering delphiniums.

46

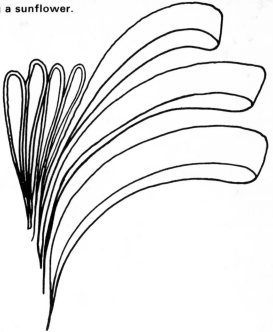

graduating them in length until the flower is 6 inches across.

Wrap the base tightly with florist's tape and continue taping downward to make a long stem. Shape the petals evenly while still damp and press the flower gently down on a board until dry. (See Color Illus. W on page 35.)

Remember, unlike paper flowers, you can rinse your corn-husk flowers under running water when they become dusty. They will stay fresh-looking much longer than paper flowers will.

Gift Wraps in Corn Husks

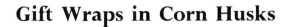

If you're concerned with the high price of gift wrappings, consider using husks to make your packages different. Make miniature wreaths or corn-husk angels for Christmas packages. Shower or wedding gifts will certainly be more original with the addition of husk flowers or a tiny parasol.

By now you probably realize you can never throw away corn husks again. You will find new ways of working with them, new uses for what you create.

Index

The woven moccasins and salt bottle on the front cover are courtesy of Buffalo Museum of Science.